**VERANDA**

# SIMPLY CHIC

## MODERN INTERIOR DESIGN

◆

*by* STEPHANIE HUNT *foreword by* STEELE THOMAS MARCOUX

HEARST
HOME

# CONTENTS

**FIRST PAGE** Gilded boiserie, plush velvets, and a French School 18th-century portrait adorn the Versailles-esque Paris flat of designer Micky Hurley.

**PREVIOUS SPREAD** Sunlight floods the family room of this Provençal-inspired villa in Los Angeles, where architect Steve Giannetti added a fully retractable glass wall for seamless indoor/outdoor living.

**LEFT** Exquisite 1930s-era carved-wood library paneling frames the birds-and-botanics beauty of a hand-painted Gracie Studio mural in a classic Connecticut Georgian designed by Ashley Whittaker.

# FOREWORD

*"Having beautiful things around you is wonderful, but living beautifully is more important."* —Suzanne Rheinstein

L EGENDARY DESIGNER Suzanne Rheinstein, who passed away in 2023, lived up to her own words in every sense—whether at home in Montecito or Los Angeles or designing homes for her beloved clients. She knew how to collaborate with architects to create something at once familiar and original. She knew how to deftly decorate a room such that her clients' most prized and personal collections shined—but never brighter than the room itself. She knew how to bring the grit of the garden inside and the polish of interiors out. She knew how to highlight the best in her clients by creating homes that reflected their dreams. And she knew how to welcome a friend, or the neighborhood, for a visit. She was, simply, *chic*.

Especially when used to describe our homes, *chic* refers to so much more than aesthetics—it's about how a home lives. Just as with an outfit, a beautiful room is not necessarily a chic one. (Some designers believe the key to creating memorable spaces is to always include at least one thing that's a little offbeat.) After all, beauty without substance or soul falls flat.

A chic home beckons with its beauty, to be sure, but it also welcomes with its warmth, delights with its charisma, and lingers on the mind with its idiosyncratic point of view. As such, chic homes know no geographic or style boundaries: A contemporary New York apartment can be as chic as an Idaho mountain lodge.

This book presents a collection of the chicest homes, from urban dwellings to island escapes. Like Rheinstein, the designers and architects featured here do so much more for their clients than buy beautiful things for their spaces. They help them live beautifully—and it shows in every room. I hope they inspire you to live beautifully, especially at home.

STEELE THOMAS MARCOUX

**RIGHT** Stately paneling gets a decidedly chic coat of lapis lacquer in this dining room with painted chevron floors inspired by a 1970s Albert Hadley room.

# INTRODUCTION

D ESPITE THE TITLE OF THIS BOOK, defining *chic* is not all that simple. Chic is sophistication and elegance, balance and ebullience. Chic is stylish and fashionable, never trendy, never trying too hard. Chic is many things, actually, but mostly it's that ineffable essence best described as "you know it when you see it." And readers will see it here, in this tour of homes in which the design, the patterns and palettes and points of view, are utterly confident and breathtakingly inspiring. They meld into a style and character that ring so instinctual and true that the chicness feels innate. Indeed, that's the beauty of elevated ease—it's authentic, alluring, and always dazzling.

Sadly, there's no fail-proof formula for chic, no YouTube tutorial to be distilled into these pages. It's a look and feel that takes intuitive talent and an accomplished eye to pull off, and it's the purview and superpower of the designers showcased here. They are masters of elegance; their designs round out the architecture and setting of each space in such a way that it evokes both harmony and delightful surprise, a sense of, *Oh, I'd like to spend time here.*

As hard as it is to pin down, chic knows no borders nor bounds, and so these pages celebrate global chic, highlighting the best of VERANDA style, from San Miguel to Montreal, from Paris to Pebble Beach, from the English Channel to the rocky coast of Maine. You'll visit metropolitan manses and country cottages, tony pieds-à-terre and woodsy lakeside cabins, because effortless elegance, can be found in any abode where warmth and welcome are paramount.

**LEFT** A sunny breakfast room by Meg Braff delivers fresh garden appeal, thanks to a classic trellis wallcovering (a Meg Braff design) and plaster-finished lantern laced with vines. For the Serge Roche-type chairs, Braff chose a linen botanical print to vary the patterns and textures in her apple green scheme.

*chapter one*

# COSMOPOLITAN EXUBERANCE

**M**ANHATTAN, MIAMI, MONTREAL, MILAN…great metropolises are the incubators of culture, our living, breathing laboratories of style. The *rues* of Paris pulse with seemingly effortless élan—even a baguette comes off as elegant. In cities, fashion, art, and design collide in a dizzying cosmopolitan collage. Wherever people and ideas congregate, where the glamorous and the gritty share cabs and crosswalks and the trendy and the traditional rub elbows, this is where chic thrives. Not surprisingly, the root of urbanity ("refinement, elegance, sophistication") is urban.

Big cities, of course, have distinct personalities and public spaces with the unique flavor, sounds, smells, and landmarks that let you know you're in New York, not London. Similarly, a well-designed home echoes the vernacular, the language spoken around it. What counts as chic in Montreal may not pass muster in Miami, but as these homes demonstrate, the core ingredients are shared: a strong point of view, authentic flavor, and soulful character.

In Paris, designer Micky Hurley went tête-à-tête with the Versailles-like opulence of his 17th-century flat, making a stately manse feasible for his family of seven. Overlooking Montreal, the architecture/design duo Les Ensembliers resurrected a convent chapel as a penthouse for Canada's former prime minister. Designer Sig Bergamin's apartment reflects the multicultural spiciness of Miami, while in Manhattan, a Flatiron district apartment and one in the legendary Carlyle are both singular odes to Big Apple magic. Meanwhile, down in jazzy New Orleans, a young family authors a new chapter in their bookstore-slash-home, perhaps creating the script for a whole new category—"literary chic."

Exuberant, sophisticated design is hardly exclusive to big cities. But the vibrancy of city life, the sensual smorgasbord of an urban center, ignites the imagination. Navigating a metropolis is rarely simple, but coming home to a stylish haven is the epitome of simply chic, and simply divine.

**LEFT** A family lounge area on the top floor gleams like a glass box, complete with panoramic views. An Alexander Calder mobile adds bright playfulness. "It's cozy, sort of like the basement of the home, but it's in the sky," says designer Max Vandal.

# MONTREAL MAGNIFIQUE

The Quebecois architecture and design duo Les Ensembliers
transform a dilapidated former chapel into an amen-worthy penthouse.

**LEFT** When Mila Mulroney, Canada's former first lady, tasked Richard Ouellette and his partner Max Vandal with converting the top floors of an old convent into a tony downtown apartment, the two set about creating an airy, sophisticated abode— formal yet animated by a lively mix of styles and art. The living room's neutral and gold palette, punctuated by silk ikat draperies and classic Corinthian molding, is an elegant backdrop for the couple's Chinese and African art.

**PAGE 12** The Mulroneys love Canadian art and have "spent their lives collecting the stories that come with each piece," says Ouellette, who ensured the double-height foyer offered plenty of gallery space, including for a tree-like sculpture by Canadian artist Laura Santini, dramatically suspended near the balustrade of the limestone stairwell.

**PAGE 13** Surrounded by parks on three sides, the penthouse is flooded with light. The dining corner of the open living space is anchored by a show-stopping antique crystal chandelier. Custom dining chairs covered in shagreen leather tone down the formality.

**LEFT** The former prime minister's study, with custom shelves for his books and photos, features plush velvet-clad sofas and chairs along with mementos of his time in office, including a Shirley Van Dusen painting of the Canadian Parliament building, which hangs above a French marble mantelpiece.

**LEFT** Cane-back chairs and an antique English breakfast table make an ideal spot for croissants and *café* in the kitchen, where copper pans shine overhead and Caesarstone countertops are both practical and stylish.

**LEFT** Canadian art enlivens every corner of the penthouse—including a bedroom hallway.

**BELOW** The 2,000-square-foot terrace overlooking the Montreal skyline and the Saint Lawrence River extends the entertaining and relaxing space, especially handy when the Mulroneys' 13 grandchildren come to visit. Chinese ceramics and pillows featuring Les Ensembliers' linen line with Brunschwig & Fils dress up the outdoor room.

**ABOVE** A medley of blues and whites creates a serene bedroom oasis, with embroidered floral draperies adding cheerful details. The goal, says Vandal, was to create "understated rooms that speak to traditional character but are still modern."

◆

*"It's all about creating little moments and building up momentum."*

—*Max Vandal*

# LUMINOUS LONDON

Designer Philip Vergeylen transforms a tired yet historic apartment into the epitome
of modern glamour and a spectacular showcase for a serious art collection.

**LEFT** A small cloakroom harbors wildlife surprises, thanks to a porcelain parrot perched atop a painted Italian chest and a pair of Napoleon III vases graced by ceramic iguanas.

**RIGHT** Vergeylen doused the dining room in luminous gold leaf hand-painted by decorative artist Henry van der Vijver, who the designer says "knocked [the gold] back with so many layers of glaze to temper it, making it glow at night." Vergeylen echoed the octagonal skylight with a similarly shaped 1970s Maison Jansen dining table.

**LEFT** Neutral drawing room walls are calm and soothing, but it took layers of scraping and distressing to achieve the texture Vergeylen desired as backdrop for his client's art, including gold-leaf iconography flanking an abstract Lucio Fontana canvas. "I like that contrast; religious works could feel too precious if not paired with something edgy," he says.

**ABOVE** Candy apple–red cabinetry holds its own against elaborate molding in this bright kitchen, flavored by geometric pattern-play on the stained-wood floors. "These are not weak rooms; we made some bold decisions," says Vergeylen.

**LEFT** Deep onyx, golds, and ruby reds give this guest room a handsome flourish. A custom striped wallcovering almost feels like wood paneling, making an inviting base layer for an early-20th-century dragon rug hung over the bed and an 18th-century oil painting above the dresser.

**ABOVE** Leopard-print walls unleash a bit of untamed verve in an otherwise buttoned-up library, where a minimalist 1970s French brass-front desk contrasts with maximalist *décollage* by Mimmo Rotella.

**RIGHT** In the primary bedroom, a bed lavishly cocooned in Pierre Frey silk taffeta with a cotton Claremont canopy is the ultimate in luxury. A vintage Chinese rug adds to the richness.

# A NEW ORLEANS PAGE-TURNER

In an 1840s townhouse where William Faulkner wrote *Soldiers' Pay*, his first novel, designers Bill Brockschmidt and Courtney Coleman continue a (non–Southern gothic) graceful storyline.

**LEFT** In a nod to New Orleans' ornamental ironwork, a privacy gate demarks the public realm of Faulkner Place bookstore from the family's living quarters, though the couple finds joy and benefit in the porousness. "Living here gives us an instant connection with the community," Permele Doyle says.

**RIGHT** In the Deep South, Faulkner is ever-present, like Spanish moss clinging to the storied oaks of New Orleans. So when Doyle and Garner Robinson made their young family's home in the 1840s townhouse where the writer once subleased the ground floor, they turned to classical design experts. "Bill and Courtney helped us see the house could be livable—that it could be what it is, and yet still be ours," says Doyle. They embraced the past in the duck-egg hues and silk drapes of the living room and added fresh vibrancy by juxtaposing antique white urns with a teal velour coffee table.

**LEFT** Like a blurred line between fact and fiction, the home's private entrance is just beyond the bookstore's office, with only a Greek revival iron gate separating the two. "There is no airtight seal between the house and the shop," Robinson says. "The air just flows right through."

**RIGHT** To denote the small dining room's function as an entertaining space, it was painted a stronger blue than the whispery hues elsewhere in the house. With a buffet of windows opening out onto the Big Easy, the room breathes the city's legendary hospitality, setting the stage for languorous dinner parties. "People don't want to leave this table," Doyle says.

◆

*"We were just so inspired by the architecture and honored to work in a house that had seen so much history." —Courtney Coleman*

**LEFT** A charming children's bedroom tucked into a dormer space is lined with bookshelves (of course!). Painting the interior of the built-in shelves a sage blue added interest and dimension.

**ABOVE** "We were just so inspired by the architecture," says Coleman, "and honored to work in a house that had seen so much history." Experts in classical proportion and traditional detailing, the designers instantly zeroed in on the house's bones. Here in the library an existing gilded mirror and fluted mantel mingle with a midcentury armchair. "We loved seeing beyond all the layers to the moldings and mantels underneath—the historic character of the space," says Doyle.

# CLASSICISM *at* THE CARLYLE

Designer Garrow Kedigian brings high-gloss wizardry to his jubilant apartment in Manhattan's legendary Carlyle Hotel.

**LEFT** A high-sheen cerulean entrance hall, iced with hand-painted gold details, is the first clue that rich color and high drama awaits. For designer Garrow Kedigian there's a why to every whimsy: he enlarged the foyer to draw one's eye directly into the living room.

**RIGHT** Living at The Carlyle on Manhattan's Upper East Side has its perks—like a private entrance to Bemelmans Bar, for one, and the occasional neighborly nod to fellow residents (hey there, Mick Jagger). But the apartment-hotel's classic iron doors and windows did it for Kedigian. His vivid citron living room is a nod to the Carlyle's iconic decorator, Dorothy Draper—her signature yellow velvet sofas (now refreshed) are still in the lobby—and the ebony molding is homage to the iron fenestration.

**LEFT** The kitchen suffered from a patchwork of cabinetry and walls, so Kedigian transformed it into a chic bar, with mural wallpaper creating a unifying narrative. "The best thing I make for dinner is reservations!" he quips. A 19th-century butler's mirror introduces gold and brass tones, subtly amplified by the kitchen's brass sheet backsplash.

**LEFT** Turning a former bedroom with fabulous daylight into his office/studio granted Kedigian the opportunity to create a red room, which he'd always found "so enticing, so beautiful. It's a severe color," he admits. "If it's too intensely red, it's jarring. I wanted it to be uplifting and rejuvenating." The final match was less crimson, more orange, the result of numerous tries.

*"I still look at those gorgeous handles on those gorgeous terrace doors and think to myself: I can't believe I get to live here!"* — *Garrow Kedigian*

**LEFT** The original wrought iron terrace doors inspired the black accents in the room adjacent to the terrace, and bold black molding throughout the apartment.

**RIGHT** This 19th-century bed was the designer's first big purchase, which he snapped up at a Montreal auction when he was just 15. A large landscape painting anchors a wall, and Greek key motifs (echoed elsewhere in the apartment) underscore Kedigian's playful classicism.

# ESPRIT *de* PARIS

Interior designer Micky Hurley embellishes an impeccably preserved
17th-century flat with a trove of art and antiques.

**PAGE 40** The entryway, with soaring walls upholstered in garnet-hued antique Venetian fabric, elicits an unequivocal *Mais oui!*, which is exactly how the owners, interior designer Micky Hurley and his wife, felt upon first seeing this flat in the city where they had long dreamed of living. "We love everything about Paris," Hurley says. "The sky, the colors, the museums, the architecture, the parks, the beauty—all of it."

**PAGE 41** Hurley, a Chilean native, and his wife, Malu, who grew up summering in Paris, had long sought a pied-à-terre in the City of Light and jumped when this one became available. In a living room corner, a citron-hued Louis XVI settee covered in antique silk creates a cozy nook, complete with a pair of Italian decoupage paintings.

**LEFT** Designed by the house architect of the Duc d'Orleans, this circa 1655 flat on the Right Bank exudes Parisian opulence. According to Hurley, "the warmth and depth that antiques give a space is immeasurable. They make it feel lived-in and personal." A pair of Louis XV fauteuils once owned by Greta Garbo flanks a tufted silk velvet sofa, while 12 marble Caesar intaglios and an oil painting of one of Hurley's ancestors grace the walls etched with elegant boiserie.

**LEFT** With five children, the Hurleys know that regal quickly meets real, but rather than go the functional route (a bunk room, say) they stayed true to the period flavor, with twin Louis XVI–style children's beds, and custom trundles to squeeze everyone in.

**RIGHT** The two-bedroom apartment had been beautifully preserved over the centuries, including an overhaul 20 years ago by designers Joseph Achkar and Michel Charrière. "They have an incomparable attention to detail," notes Hurley. In the primary bedroom, an ornate marble fireplace, intact original Zuber wallcovering in the iconic Petit Parque pattern, and Versailles-style oak parquet floors evoke the grandeur of past époques.

*"Each object we brought in has a sense of importance, no matter how big or small."* —*Micky Hurley*

# MAXIMAL MIAMI HEAT

Triumphant colors and whimsical pattern play are Brazilian designer
Sig Bergamin's calling cards in this game-on Miami apartment.

*"I love to mix everything together. That's my concept: mix, mix, mix."*

—Sig Bergamin

**LEFT** Boisterous prints covering every imaginable surface is designer Sig Bergamin's signature, fully evident in this vivacious Miami apartment where he layers pattern upon pattern with riotous hues, like the deep ruby daybed. "My client loves design and to be surrounded by lots of fabrics," Bergamin says. The living room's thickly textured beige rug took a year and a half to fabricate. "The rug is like the sand," he says. "I like when there's little contrast between outside and inside."

**PAGE 46** In the foyer, a bone inlay dresser showcases intricate detail while Islamic-inspired ironwork doors hint at the home's global influences.

**PAGE 47** Bergamin is fearless with color, welcoming the bold and bright in his "more the merrier" philosophy. Here a profusion of pillows and tasseled bolsters play well with bone-inlay furnishings and Florida-inspired coral accents.

**RIGHT** In the dining room, a bespoke tiled wall offers a graphic, glossy backdrop for a rosette-patterned banquette. Bergamin found the ornate chandelier in a Brazilian antiques shop.

**ABOVE** Various shades of coral and red enliven a guest room, which Bergamin wrapped in a charcoal sisal wallcovering. The effect is Marrakesh meets Miami meets tropical retreat. "He has a very open mind, always wanting to learn about other ways to understand beauty," says the homeowner.

**RIGHT** Sweet dreams are all but guaranteed, thanks to coverlets trimmed in pale blue evoking azure skies, while paisley drips from canopies to upholstered headboards to the rug, bringing a calm unity to the hushed bedroom.

# FLAWLESS *in* FLATIRON

Designer Robert Passal brings serene posh
and sophisticated eclecticism to a historic apartment
building in New York's Flatiron district.

**LEFT** The owners "wanted little reading nooks and places to hang out or have a conversation," says Passal, who commissioned Vietnamese artist Francis Nguyen to paint the folding screen with ethereal abstract nudes for a quiet corner, adding a splash of soothing color. "It was a way to create a moment without it being over-the-top."

**RIGHT** When a Denver-based couple found their ideal Manhattan pied-à-terre in a 1912 high rise, they turned to designer Robert Passal to give the three-bedroom apartment the updates and TLC it needed. "The idea was to make the space feel approachable yet artful, using a mix of eras and aesthetics," says Passal. The living room's muted palette invites the couple's art to shine, including a still life by Alec Soth flanked by a pair of 19th-century Italian sconces and a clay visage sculpture by Picasso.

**LEFT** Although the 3,200-square-foot apartment allowed for ample entertaining spaces, a large formal dining room was not high on the owners' list of priorities. Instead, an oak hall table showcasing art books and collectibles can expand for seating up to eight, when needed. Otherwise, the apartment's optimal proximity to Flatiron nightlife and restaurants suffices. "You know, I'm not coming to New York to cook for 20," the owner says.

**RIGHT** A streamlined kitchen, featuring sculptural antique brass counter stools upholstered in pistachio leather, gets warmth from natural materials like wood and marble. Passal stripped the floors and refinished them using a matte wax oil that reveals more of the wood's natural graining and color variations.

**RIGHT** In the marble-floored entryway, the designer brought in artisans to embellish the walls with fluted plaster, making a high-impact statement. "It's all hand-troweled," he says. "That was two months' worth of work."

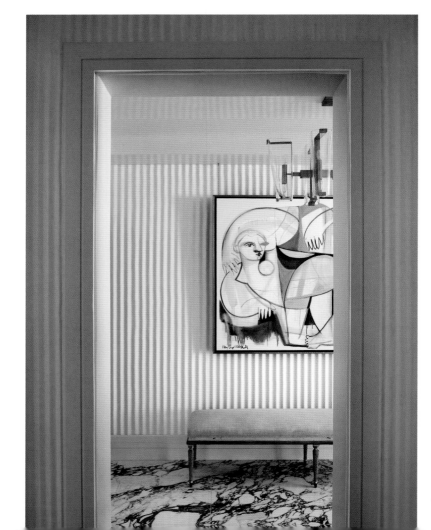

**LEFT** A handcrafted, pearl-like lighting fixture by Canadian designer Larose Guyon—the husband's surprise housewarming-slash-birthday gift to his wife—bejewels a deep soaking tub. "Pearls are my favorite," she says. "It not only made the bathroom, I think it made the whole apartment. I mean, it's just magnificent, isn't it?"

**RIGHT** The primary bedroom is a dreamscape of decadent sorbet hues— a beguiling backdrop for an oil painting by Cynthia Packard. Passal chose a flared-headboard bed and found an antique Swedish crystal chandelier to add elements of romance and quiet drama.

◆

*"The apartment wasn't meant to be splashy. We had a distinct look we were going for, which was calm and clean."* —Robert Passal

*chapter two*

# IN-TOWN ELEGANCE

T O BE IN TOWN is to be among the familiar, the friendly. While big cities can be both exhilarating and daunting, town is more easily embraceable. It's human-scale and welcoming, and its residences, like the ones here, reflect that in their comfortable confidence. Home may be where the heart is, but there's a reason we call wherever it is we hail from our "home*town*."

Homes in towny locales typically have more space than their corollaries in more contained urban enclaves, which gives designers the dynamism and roominess to reflect vivid personalities and varying moods, often under one roof. Here we find stately Georgians and stalwart Colonials, a Provence-inspired Los Angeles showstopper, and even a Long Island ranch redo. Many are crowned by shade trees and have yards and verdant gardens, and their interiors blossom with brilliance, bringing hints of the outdoors in. And when pushing beyond nature's palette, designers like Meg Braff with her chartreuse living room or Ashley Whittaker with a lavishly lacquered peacock blue dining room, are fearless with color. There's a mastery of scale and balance that distills even the loftiest rooms—like an open two-story kitchen by Steven Gambrel— into warm, joyful spaces.

These designers go to town with elegance and sophistication that feels equally at home in Connecticut or California. In this respect chic knows no bounds, because it's not style for style's sake but rather a reflection of personality—of objects, art, and people much loved, and how all these live and interact in a space that shapes who we are, or who we will grow to be. As designer David Netto put it, these houses are "a portrait of these clients, or of who they had not become yet, still asleep."

**LEFT** Celebrating California's indoor/outdoor lifestyle, designers Steve and Brooke Giannetti borrowed the limestone and stucco vernacular of an old French courtyard for this entryway, complete with an antique fountain.

# PROVENÇAL PATINA

Team Giannetti brings a bit of Southern France to
Southern California in this garden-centric Los Angeles home.

**ABOVE** For this architecture/design duo, a 16th-century
Flemish tapestry is right at home with cozy, more
contemporary George Smith sofas and celadon-cushioned
chairs in this family room for clients in Los Angeles.
"We're combining the best of the modern world with
the best of the Old World in a way that feels authentic,"
says Steve Giannetti.

**RIGHT** Painted wicker chairs and a simple trestle table
underscore the breakfast room's garden connection,
with French doors that make alfresco entertaining or
morning coffee an easy option.

**LEFT** A mural by decorative painter Maria Trimbell gives the dining room an elegant woodland air, making it feel like an extension of the outdoors. Soft wood tones and chairs in mossy velvet whisper echoes of the natural world.

**ABOVE** The central staircase with stucco walls and a ficus tree overlooks planted ivy and was "designed to conjure an old French courtyard," says Steve Giannetti. A two-story bank of glass-and-steel windows invites a cascade of California sunshine.

**LEFT** A buffet of windows serves up ample light in the kitchen, where a white oak and Calacatta marble island is flanked by linen-covered barstools.

**RIGHT** A sun-drenched second-floor sitting room is bathed in a soothing robin's-egg blue, with velvet tufted ottomans in the rosy peach of a robin's breast. Brooke Giannetti's goal was to create a feeling of calm "through the senses—with the sound of water, the scent of roses, the gentle, dappled shade from the trees, all of that," she says.

**RIGHT** A melody of classic furnishings and neutrals underscores the formal living room's graceful sophistication, with French doors opening to the garden.

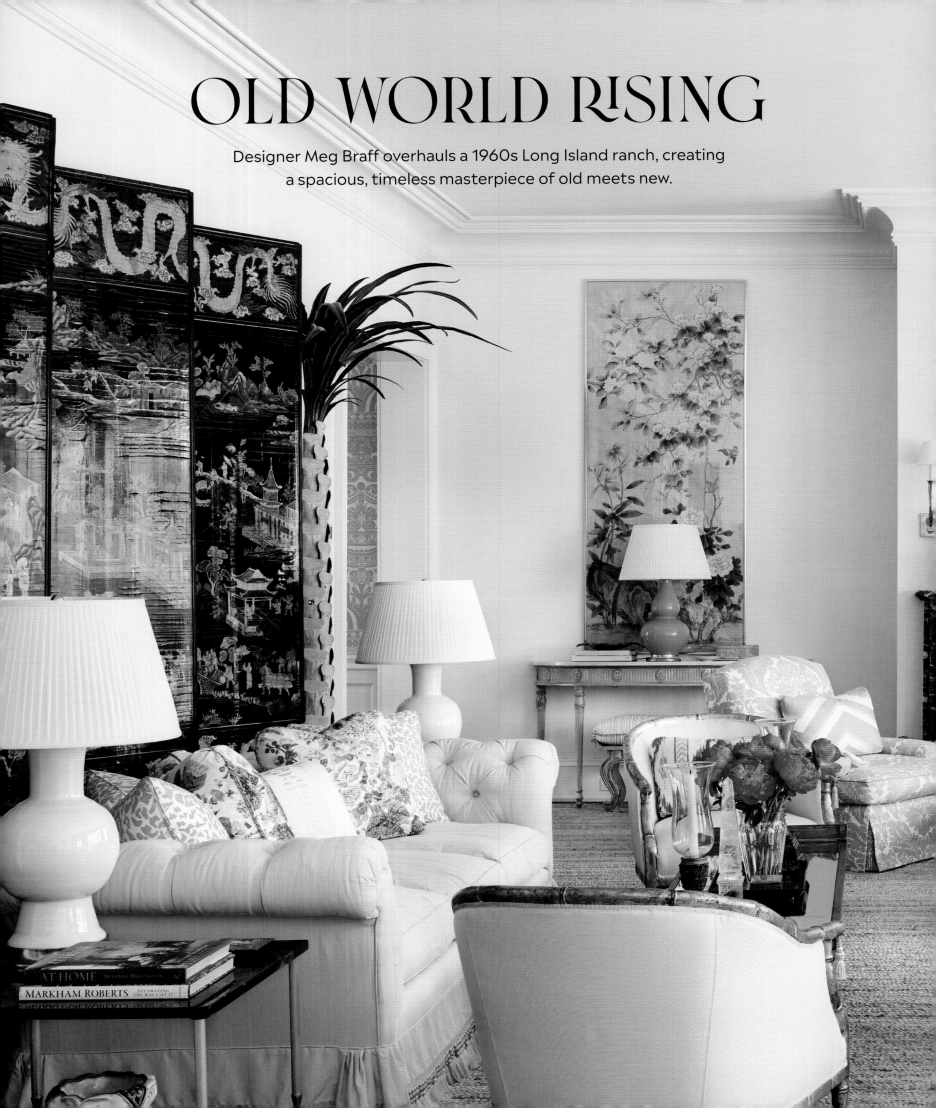

# OLD WORLD RISING

Designer Meg Braff overhauls a 1960s Long Island ranch, creating
a spacious, timeless masterpiece of old meets new.

**PAGES 66-67** Homeowner and designer Meg Braff wields unabashed color in giving a former modest ranch an opulent upgrade in which gilt George III mirrors and antiques are comfortable. An imposing Coromandel screen highlights a living room filled with French and English furniture and porcelain galore—"all my favorite things," says the designer, who found the Belgian marble mantels at auction.

**ABOVE** Antique French armchairs accompany an entryway console in the main hall, where the strong, classic lines of a Louis XVI mirror are softened by a flock of vintage bird prints. "We wanted it to feel like a house built in the early 1930s, like it had always been here," says Braff.

**RIGHT** "I love walking from room to room and experiencing how the different tones work together, like they're speaking to each other in a beautiful, congenial way," says Braff. The designer painted the original paneled library walls in a vibrant chartreuse. Blue accents and leopard print on the cane-back armchairs and pillows keep the conversation lively.

**LEFT** "I try be very thoughtful about threading color through the rooms," says Braff, who weaves in green from the adjacent spaces via the dining room's green apple valance and drapes. A black lacquer buffet and faux-painted Regency chairs add heft and interest, balancing the formality of the Baltic crystal chandelier.

**ABOVE** In a sitting room, Braff playfully mixes materials and patterns, starting with contemporary yet classic Katie Ridder wallpaper. On the James Mont–style midcentury horseshoe chairs, timeless black-and-white ticking cozies up to an apricot velvet sofa, and a rattan chandelier adds earthy informality.

**RIGHT** A dramatic Schumacher wallcovering ensconces the primary bedroom in a colorful bamboo canopy, while a neobaroque Serge Roche–inspired bed in bright white punctuates the surrounding pattern with sturdy glamour.

# TONY *and* UNTAMED

Designer Ashley Whittaker enlivens a stately Connecticut
Georgian with spirited color and a family-forward playfulness.

**PAGE 74** Original millwork glossed in a brilliant peacock blue is a show-stopping backdrop for a collection of vintage blue-and-white porcelain. A painted chevron floor adds pizzazz.

**PAGE 75** Whittaker mixes in contemporary statements, like a Robert Motherwell abstract over the mantel and mod tiger-print velvet chairs, to energize the library with its 1930s carved wood paneling.

**LEFT** The designer juxtaposes a wool-covered banquette with spirited Pierre Frey wallpaper in the game room of this Georgian manse. Architect George Knight partnered with Whittaker to create an ambiance he describes as "more familial than formal."

**RIGHT** Checkerboard floors and a punchy geometric-floral pattern on the counter stools add flavor to a traditional white kitchen. Whittaker summons the dining room's peacock blue with pendants by Charles Edwards. Though a functional work space, the kitchen "is meant to be in the foreground rather than the background," says Knight.

"*The living room should be as comfortable when entertaining…for cocktails as it is for…sitting around the fireplace.*" —*Ashley Whittaker*

**LEFT** An entrance hall features a majestic double-height stairwell, a hand-painted Gracie Studio mural wallcovering, and an elegant scroll arm settee.

**LEFT** Grand Georgian moldings give Old World distinction to this 30-foot-long living room, yet Whittaker tones down the formality with upholstery pattern play: A whimsical green and a medley of blue botanicals, ikats, and chevrons are all set against soothing, creamy Venetian plaster walls.

**RIGHT** Whittaker layers textures and details in this dreamy bedroom, where a tufted upholstered bed is draped by a double-sided baldachin and topped with scalloped-edge linens. The Hollyhock wallcovering is by Lee Jofa.

# PERMISSION GRANTED

Designer David Netto loves hearing yes, especially from clients willing to give an old Colonial all they've got.

**LEFT** When a young couple asked Netto to reimagine this "sweet 1930s Colonial" in Connecticut, he respected the budget discussed with the husband—until the wife intervened. Don't mind him; show me your best ideas, she said. "That's when I got all my yeses," says Netto. "That's how we get a Picasso plate mounted next to a canoe paddle," he says of the stairwell gallery, complete with Audubon watercolors.

**RIGHT** Chocolaty brown walls in full gloss give the dining room immediate decadence, while wicker chairs around a round table add casual flair. Netto pares down the decor with bold form (plaster cone hanging light) and simple touches (red sconces).

**LEFT** Netto appreciated the "intimate scale of the rooms," including the homey kitchen, where 19th-century Portuguese tilework steals the show and an old-school copper pot collection hangs above contemporary Scandinavian bent birch counter stools.

**LEFT** Getting the green light from his clients led to "elevated touches" like the reclaimed honed Nero Marquina marble floors in the sunny family room, says Netto, where he gave the ceiling a coat of sky blue.

**LEFT** In keeping with the cozy Colonial-era feel, Netto covered walls and windows in the same Bennison Fabrics pattern. A yellow butterfly cabinet topped with antique agate vases adds sunny cheer.

**RIGHT** Netto loves a mix of high and low, especially in a home for a young family. The living room's woven rattan chairs are juxtaposed with a vintage Louis XV limestone mantelpiece, over which hangs a Georges Braque lithograph.

**RIGHT** In the family room, to complement knotty pine walls and raffia wallcovering, Netto and architect Sam Mitchell added vintage farmhouse beams "that should have always been there," says the designer.

# REGENCY REBORN

Designer Steven Gambrel infuses youthful vibrancy into a New Jersey abode,
reinvigorating its Regency glamour and Art Deco allure.

**PAGE 86** "The idea was to use the house's history as inspiration but not make it too literal, too luxe. We wanted it to feel young and relevant," says Gambrel, who revitalized this circa 1928 New Jersey home for a young family. In the entry stairwell, light from an arched window touches a tufted leather bench and lithographs from Le Corbusier's *Le Poème de l'angle droit*.

**PAGE 87** The designer turned the original entry hall into an orangery-inspired conservatory, opening to the terrace. Potted trees and a quartet of mirrors surround a hefty stone table that doubles as a bar when the owners entertain.

**LEFT** Retaining hints of the spacious living room formality of yore, Gambrel designed intimate seating configurations "to speak to each other." Windows and doors trimmed in steely gray and strié walls add definition and warmth to the muted palette.

**LEFT** Working with architect Eric J. Smith, Gambrel turned a former staff wing into an airy two-story kitchen with clerestory windows. "Its volume comes as a bit of a surprise," says Smith. A striking gunmetal-and-brass hood and indigo green marble island set the stage for handsome gray millwork and gold leather seating. "I like to make kitchens equally as complex and layered" as other rooms in the house, says Gambrel.

**RIGHT** No stuffiness allowed in this library. "Wood paneling gives it old-school resonance, while the youthfulness comes from the intense satin-brushed teal and cinnabar lacquer," says Gambrel. A vintage brass U-shaped writing desk speaks to the home's Deco era.

**ABOVE** Dark wood floors and double vanities surround the primary bath's centerpiece, a double-ended soaking tub. An understated Deco vibe emanates from vanity sconces with hexagonal glass panes.

**RIGHT** Texture is the main course in the dining room, where Gambrel gridded natural Barkskin walls to mimic stone, and a sisal rug grounds the Jazz Age glamour of the tufted banquette.

**LEFT** In the garden room, a custom-painted baby grand piano adds a fresh tune. "I realize it's not entirely in the school of good taste," admits Gambrel of the painted Steinway, "but it's really interesting and unexpected."

# chapter three

# COASTAL GLAMOUR

A LONG THE COAST, chic ripples along its own wavelength. It is the sun glinting off the water—a disco ball of dazzle. It's the gentle pulse of tides lapping on a shore. Here, chic reflects the mysterious way life at the coast dials us down to something essential, the way water and light dissolve into a tonic of relaxed gloriousness. Whether on Monterey Bay or Lake Michigan, in Nova Scotia or Naples, Florida, the particular pizzazz of each coastal home is distinct, but this sense of glamorous ease is a common thread.

In these coastal beauties, you won't find an overload of shells or nautical tropes; nothing screams *beach*. They tend to be elegant in an understated way that could be at home in any landscape, but there is that hint of fresh salty breeze, of take-your-sandals-off-and-pour-a-cocktail—signaling that these are homes designed for entertaining, relaxing, and savoring. These rooms invite the spirit to slip into another gear, to gently coast, as it were, which life along the shore beckons us to do.

In the remote reaches of the East Coast, architect and designer Philip Mitchell gives love and luster to centuries-old plank floors and exposed beams to reinvigorate an 18th-century Nova Scotia beauty with newfound shimmer. Old Florida enchantment gets a posh, sublime gleam with Bobby McAlpine's transcendent architecture and designer Susan Ferrier's suave touch, while on the West Coast, designer Mary McDonald balances quiet tones and big wow in a Pebble Beach château. As Florida native Celerie Kemble demonstrates, pink is always on point for a coastal palette and dashes of whimsy add waves of delight. And for a woodsy cabin along Lake Michigan, Amy Meier proves that down-to-earth is its own kind of elegance, sometimes all the more so when it's a little rough around the edges. These abodes that hug the coastline are grounded in character; they know who they are, which makes chic feel natural.

**LEFT** A dining terrace overlooking Mecox Bay in the Hamptons features an antique rattan table and chairs, and in the distance, a cast bronze and gilt garden sculpture halos bayberry hedges.

# ALL THAT GLITTERS

Designer Alex Papachristidis gives summer house style a gilded makeover in this art-filled Hamptons home awash in dazzling seaside light.

LEFT The entryway gives immediate clues of ornate delight, thanks to a hand-molded gold ceramic chandelier by Eve Kaplan. Plaster honeycomb artwork by Sophie Coryndon further underscores the shimmery welcome.

PAGE 98 Hand-painted waves on a Gracie Studio wallcovering float down the main corridor of this Long Island home designed by Alex Papachristidis.

PAGE 99 When his sister is the client, Papachristidis knows he can take gilded to the max. "What Alex understands is that I'm a romantic. I love things that are aesthetically glamorous," says home-owner Ophelia Rudin, whose living room is aglow with white lacquered walls and brass strapping, and jewelry-like bronze disc lighting by Hervé Van der Straeten.

LEFT A gilded rock form table crafted by Eve Kaplan through Gerald Bland is the dining room's mother lode, while a Swedish bronze and crystal chandelier dazzles from above. Radiant heated Jerusalem limestone floors here and throughout the house give balance to the home's metallic sheen.

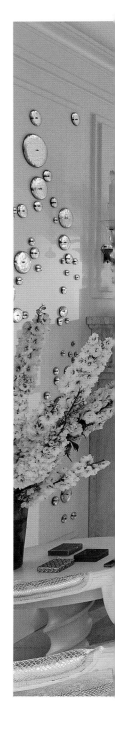

**LEFT** Even the smallest nooks get the full glam treatment, as this tucked-away desk demonstrates. Verre églomisé panels by glass artist Miriam Ellner elevate the cozy work space.

**BELOW** "Gold leaf" takes on new meaning in this gilded forest-themed guest room, where a white-plaster woodland canopy bed was inspired by Pauline de Rothschild's Château Mouton.

ABOVE Constellations of silvered glass bubbles by artist Rob Wynne dance across the primary bedroom walls, while a hefty gold desk by Chris Schanck anchors a light-filled corner. The home, on a parcel once owned by Richard Bach, author of *Jonathan Livingston Seagull*, seems to impart a Jonathan-inspired flight of fancy.

◆

*"Every sheet, every napkin, every dish—everything shimmers of precious metal."*

—*Alex Papachristidis*

# NOVA SCOTIA CHARM

In a dreamy seaside village, designer and architect Philip Mitchell
channels his passion for history, reviving a 1795 home into a gleaming getaway.

**ABOVE** Nooks and crannies galore were part of the charm that seduced the Canadian designer and his husband into tackling a to-the-studs restoration of this 18th-century cottage in Chester, Nova Scotia.

**LEFT** Tongue-and-groove paneling and exposed beams nod to the cottage's historic character in the sun-washed living room. "I'd never been to any of the Maritime Provinces, but we totally fell in love," says Mitchell. The duo stumbled upon and rescued this seaside "Colonial mishmash" of a house that had suffered severe water damage and had been targeted by developers for demolition.

**PAGE 104** The two-and-a-half-year restoration entailed dismantling the entire structure; numbering, cataloging, and reusing everything they could; and reprising the original footprint and style. The entryway's marble floor includes an inscription (1795) denoting when the cottage was originally built.

**PAGE 105** Gorgeous wide-plank floors feature restored wooden boards of varying lengths mixed together. "That's why they have this beautiful character," says Mitchell, who reveled in the craftsmanship of area artisans—a legacy of shipbuilding trades.

**LEFT** The kitchen has ample old-salt ambiance, with marine ceiling lights and a rustic hemlock island paired with funkier lilac counter stools. Softness reigns over a leather banquette curled around a hardy wood table thanks to the Urban Electric Co. custom ikat pendant.

**RIGHT** Mitchell delights in adding to family heirloom collections, including these Limoges fish plates displayed in the cottage's servery.

◆

*"We totally fell in love. Chester [Nova Scotia] has historic integrity and unbelievably friendly people. It's a little slice of heaven."*
—Philip Mitchell

**LEFT** Sweet slumber is ensured in this tucked-away sleeping alcove, an extra haven for guests in the beadboard dressing room.

**RIGHT** A third-floor guest bedroom furnished with an enchanting mélange of Swedish, French, and English antiques opens to a harbor-front roof deck.

**LEFT** Mitchell and his husband have made fast friends among the seaside village's 1,500 residents, whom they entertain around the stone fireplace under the outdoor pergola. "We love the wide mix of people, from socialites to fishermen," he says.

# NAPLES ANEW

For a Florida rebuild, architect Bobby McAlpine and designer Susan Ferrier celebrate the sublime power of a muted palette.

**LEFT** With couture-esque details, a crisp stucco exterior is like a "clean garment," says McAlpine. He took cues from 1930s abstracted classicism in designing this new home on Naples Bay, replacing the homeowners' mold-wrecked prior residence. Sculpted hedges and topiaries add drama and tailored detail.

**RIGHT** By rebuilding fresh rather than renovating, McAlpine had leeway to shift the home closer to the water and expand the "pageantry" of a more spacious entryway, with twin staircases rippling down like water. It projects "a glamour that can transport you, like you've gone from Naples to Paris," he says.

**ABOVE** Ferrier's monochrome tones are elevated and "emotionally uncluttered," she says. Symmetry and refined finishes hew to the aesthetic, while white oak floors in the dining room and adjacent living room lend a soft, earthy warmth.

**RIGHT** Ferrier bookends the elongated living room with twin seating areas and fashions an ethereal backdrop out of antiqued mirrors atop hand-painted grisaille wallpaper by Ananbô.

*"I wanted it to almost feel like an embassy, to elevate the feeling and make you want to hold your back straight as you approach."*

—Bobby McAlpine

**ABOVE** The family room is a sleek, gleaming retreat with dark walls and tray ceiling, an example of McAlpine's couture details. A luminous titanium-coated steel wall sculpture by John Franzen adds movement and drama.

**RIGHT** The primary bedroom suite includes his-and-her baths, both awash in luxury and glamour. This shrine of lustrous marble (walls and flooring) features a fluted vanity and Hollywood-esque chandelier.

**BELOW** The couple's intimately scaled bedroom with fully upholstered walls can be curtained off, completely blacking out the world. "You can close yourself up in a fabric box," says McAlpine. "It's like having a sleep mask on."

# DEEPWATER DREAM

Designer Celerie Kemble doubles down on Old Florida enchantment for a
Naples abode overlooking tangly mangroves and the deep channel of Gordon Pass.

PAGE 118 A native Floridian turned New Yorker, Celerie Kemble was in her element designing this abode overlooking Gordon Pass and the nature preserve beyond. "Every aspect is oriented toward the water," says Kemble, who infused indigo prints and vintage teak accents into the open-air sunroom.

PAGE 119 The pink exterior hue, "the color of conch," was a no-brainer for Kemble, who trimmed British Colonial–inspired arches in white. The breezy pavilion's concrete tiles are cool on the feet, and black trimmed pillows add just enough punctuation.

**LEFT** Balancing out all the bright, airy spaces, a quiet den offers a darker retreat, albeit with tropical nods, including a dried water hyacinth wallcovering and woven textures in the side table and lampshade.

**LEFT** The dining room, with large-scale artwork crafted from Marseilles Opera House backdrops, is Kemble's aria to the distinctive and dramatic. Cane panels in ebonized mahogany frames hearken to native materials, and Jamaican mahogany chairs add a touch of formality while echoing an island vibe.

**ABOVE** Happy hour at this quaint bar is full of locals, complete with Florida-made spirits and plenty of native fauna, including a carved wooden alligator, sea fan, varnished turtle shell, and whelks.

**RIGHT** Indoor/outdoor living—and sleeping—is seamless thanks to a fully retractable glass door in the primary bedroom, where a simple black iron four-poster bed is cradled in creamy white linens.

RIGHT Given her Florida roots, Kemble understands water's powerful allure. A knife-edge pool flush with the coral stone deck serves as a teaser for the waterway it overlooks, while abundant areca, fishtail, and cat palms give a lush backdrop and privacy.

# MONTEREY BAY MAGIC

Designer Mary McDonald fills a grand Pebble Beach château
with glorious light, layered touches, and modern livability.

**LEFT** McDonald was tasked with breathing fresh life into a dated and drab Normandy-style château with a decidedly non-drab view of Monterey Bay. The library is a study in ethereal pearly grays. "We wanted it to look layered and collected, and for that you need a variety of materials and finishes," McDonald says.

**ABOVE** A custom Gracie Studio papered screen defines an intimate seating area in the oversize living room. While the château's 12,000 square feet give the family with young triplets plenty of roaming room, McDonald also looked to create inviting nooks.

**PAGE 126** Perched on a Pebble Beach cliffside, the home's outdoor entertaining and living areas are enjoyed year-round thanks to a stone firepit and glass wind/spray screens.

**PAGE 127** "The house just needed to be lightened up. We took it to a contemporary, clean version. I call it lightened French," says McDonald, who showcases light in a limestone entry-cum-solarium, with obelisk garden sculptures and very happy orchids.

**ABOVE** With her urbane sensibility, McDonald imbues a soft glow of classic elegance throughout the home. Reproduction Louis XVI chairs surround an oval walnut dining table, while an ornate chandelier commands attention.

**RIGHT** The primary bedroom is a symphony of subtle chic, with layers of texture and a poster bed that makes a clean-lined statement "without any colorful noise," says McDonald. The immense gilded bronze chandelier, however, is a gloriously unsubtle bow to the home's Gallic influence.

# LAKESIDE ALLURE

On the shores of Lake Michigan, designer Amy Meier embraces authenticity, creating a quiet vacation cabin for a family of five and their future generations.

**PAGE 132** For a family's lakeside summer outpost, Meier and architect Matt Rossetti took cues from the property's former life of disjointed outbuildings. They created a rustic main lodge with mod breezeway connections to distinct "cabins" serving as kids' bedrooms and guest quarters.

**PAGE 133** The homeowners requested that Meier preserve a rugged camp feel, with a preference for old over new. "The rustier and crustier the better," says Meier, who used a reclaimed timber header and salvaged bricks for the main living space's fireplace and nestled a reading and conversation corner along a soaring wall of windows.

**LEFT** Meier juxtaposes stone and wood, glass and steel in a combination "that feels old but fresh," says the designer, who intentionally left the plastered wall above the fireplace blank, "so light dances above it." Despite the great room's soaring ceiling and alluring interior, the wooded lake view takes center stage.

**ABOVE** Walnut milled from a local downed tree tops an island painted deep green and bookended by open shelving for collections of splatterware and copperware. Belgian Blue Stone tiles paired with a timber header create an earthy backsplash.

**RIGHT** Tucked behind the kitchen's backsplash/faux wall, a butler's pantry provides a light-drenched prep and flower-arranging station. Cabinets in a bandsawn knotty white oak gain patina over time.

**LEFT** Old brick, reclaimed barn wood, and barrel-aged bourbon make a satisfying cocktail in this earthy hideaway bar, where stitched leather stools and vintage Swedish lamps beckon guests to gather round.

**RIGHT** Guest room walls hide insulation behind unfinished planks to emulate the original guest cabin's quaint but often chilly, raw simplicity. "I love that everything's a little funky, a little off," says the homeowner.

◆

*"We didn't want a fancy house. The lake is our place to turn off and read a book…a place to simplify amid life's complexity."* —Homeowner

**LEFT** Reclaimed barn wood cloaks the primary bedroom with woodsy warmth, and an antique Gustavian writing desk awaits journaling. "We wanted the furniture and fabrics to look like we brought them from my grandmother's lake house, circa 70 years ago," the homeowner says.

**ABOVE** R&R is at the ready on this breezy screened porch, where a vintage French chaise and bar cart await. Antique brick flooring adds pattern, texture, and all-weather durability.

*chapter four*

# COUNTRYSIDE CALLING

THE MESMERIZING TIMELESSNESS of old stone walls. The romance of winding roads, rambling hedges, and wildflower gardens. Tidy vineyards and tangled vines, rivers slowly flowing with intoxicating insouciance, mountain chalets with timber frame reminders of the ancient craft of creating shelter. Where city lines blur away and the countryside beckons, time and imagination pull us into another realm. A realm where centuries-old manors still marvel; where estates long past their heyday whisper, *What if?*; where, under the sure hand of gifted designers, memory, dreams, and beloved possessions are layered into spaces that breathe like the landscape.

Here's a warm welcome into incredible country homes, from the English Channel to California's Russian River Valley, that manage to both honor their particular sense of history and place and transport us to new dimensions of inspired design. Checks, stripes, and bold patterns repeatedly come into play— echoing the rhythm of hill and dale (and just classic good taste). There's no forced effort to be chic. As decorator and homeowner Esther Cayzer-Colvin puts it, "I'm never making a statement." Rather, in designing her home in the county of Wiltshire in southern England, tucked among hedges of yew and beech, she's honoring "the simplicity" of a country house.

For designer Philip Gorrivan, a 1750s Colonial in the picturesque Berkshires foothills is a symphony of symmetry, with its creaky wide-plank floors and steep, narrow stairwell. Restoring it with a preservation mindset was equally an act of love and restraint—"it couldn't be too perfect," he says. Enticed by a crumbling English manor, designer Richard Smith "let the house speak to us," he says, "allowing it to come back to life in an unhurried and thoughtful way." In Sun Valley, Idaho, designer Mark D. Sikes meshes Western ruggedness with refined polish to create chic high-altitude delight. And in California's wine country, designer Ken Fulk reimagines a famed family compound, inspired by undulating "vineyards, cycling along winding roads, sun-drenched afternoons by the pool, harvest celebrations." In other words, pure country gold.

**LEFT** A late-17th-century English manor surrounded by gardens in a quaint Wiltshire village could be a *Downton Abbey* backdrop or a set for the next Jane Austen film. Its charm and romance inspired the DIY decorating of British countrywoman Esther Cayzer-Colvin.

# A WILTSHIRE WONDER

An air of English aristocracy breezes through decorator and homeowner Esther Cayzer-Colvin's redo of a centuries-old country estate, with fresh breaths of her easygoing, elevated style.

**PAGE 142** Cayzer-Colvin's decorating DNA (her grandmother Nancy Lancaster co-owned Colefax and Fowler) is evident throughout this classic-meets-comfortable eight-bedroom manse. Front hall chest and chairs are from her grandparents' Oxfordshire estate, where Winston Churchill retreated on weekends during World War II.

**PAGE 143** "Decorating is my form of creativity—I love fiddling around with color," says Cayzer-Colvin, who dressed the drawing room windows in Italian-strung linen curtains and chose a bold, buoyant Howard & Sons fabric for the ottoman. "If one person does a house, you feel it has their signature and everything fits."

**ABOVE** Cayzer-Colvin mixed greens with a friend who's a specialist decorative painter until she landed on the cooking-apple shade she once saw in a photograph. A medley of patterns, stripes, and artwork from the family's collection come together to form a harmonious whole.

**RIGHT** Velvet-on-silk curtains enliven the vibrant dining room, with distressed leather chairs and walls dished up in an artful mix of portraits and porcelain.

**LEFT** In the sunny pantry, a collection of pumpkin ceramics and books wait for their moment. A scallop-edged roman shade ties in the ubiquitous upbeat apple green.

**ABOVE** The staying power of a cheerful check and of heirloom beds—some things never go out of style.

**LEFT** Surrounded by four acres of gardens, the country manor offers numerous delightful, rambling outdoor rooms to explore, including this allée of hornbeam trees and yew hedges in the front garden.

**RIGHT** A replica of the Garrick Bed from the Victoria and Albert Museum is the crown jewel of the primary bedroom, where fringes mix with floral prints and a gathering of vintage botanicals.

**RIGHT** A claw-foot tub in a quaint nook awaits in what Cayzer-Colvin dubbed "the 50-pence bathroom," because the plumber wedged in a 50-pence coin to keep the cistern level.

# ALPINE WARMTH

Designer Mark D. Sikes embellishes the Western kitsch of a mountain cabin with European sensibilities and cozy touchstones.

**LEFT** A Dutch door and dialogue of blue and red announce lively whimsy from square one of the checkerboard entryway.

**RIGHT** "As a designer it's always a joy to work on a project that is so atypical," says Sikes of this classic Adirondack that's slightly, and delightfully, out of place in Sun Valley. "A house this whimsical gives you a good bit of liberty." Still, he toned down the camp with his signature layering of chintz, ikat, stripes, and wicker, avoiding cliché and amplifying a "moodier, warmer feeling."

**LEFT** A sweet marriage of red-and-blue stripes and Indian floral print hugs the dining chairs, while Sikes chose a woven barrel light by Soane Britain as an earthy yet updated statement piece.

**LEFT** Because this is their full-time residence and they're a nature-loving family with two children, the owners steered clear of anything "that will look dated down the road. It's classic but executed in a way that still feels fresh and new," says the homeowner. The kitchen's cascade of light reflects on the Delft tile backsplash, with an island painted a woodsy gray-green.

COUNTRYSIDE CALLING   153

**LEFT** "The magic of playing with so much texture and novelty is the repetition of things, whether it's using the same fabric in different places or linking pieces together with trim and other detailing," says Sikes, a devotee of blue and white, which reign in the bedroom and are sprinkled throughout the home.

**BELOW** Though it looks out on a Western mountain vista, this timeless guest bedroom could just as easily be on the Upper East Side. Sikes's mastery of the tailored touch is evident in the upholstered headboard and bench and the silk-and-linen canopy.

**ABOVE** Sikes doesn't let high altitude sway him from more sea-level elements, like a sea-grass wallcovering and rattan chairs. A slight hint of Moroccan influence in the cabinet millwork adds an unexpected touch.

◆

*"Some people might be scared to layer all of this together, but these clients had no trepidation when it came to color and texture."*

—*Mark D. Sikes*

# MANOR MARVEL

On a verdant bluff above the English Channel, textile designer
Richard Smith rescues a crumbling estate, turning it into
a living laboratory for experimenting with color and pattern.

PAGE 156 "Fairlight Place is a handsome and unpretentious manor house happy in its own skin," says Smith of the "romantic 17th-century wreck." Smith and his partner loved back to life this worn sandstone structure surrounded by a 15-foot wall and gardens during a nearly 15-year restoration.

PAGE 157 A Victorian tented cabana in the foyer lends festive flair, and English garden flowers give a Sussex welcome. The couple spent four years on the exterior before even beginning on the interiors. "We wanted to take our time, let the house speak to us, and allow it to come back to life in an unhurried and thoughtful way," Smith says.

LEFT The parlor's inglenook hearth gets constant use on chilly winter nights along the coast, and coziness abounds as a mix of prints and patterns reflects Smith's love of textiles.

*"For centuries this house stood ruggedly resilient to the coastal temperament, yet there was so much to rescue. And it has repaid us a hundredfold the love and thought we have put in."* —*Richard Smith*

◆

**LEFT** An old stone wall ensconces the gardens that local horticultural expert James Horner landscaped with yew and wildflowers. On Smith's afternoon "commute" from his studio—a former cart shed set into the wall—he often pauses for tea on the vintage Brighton café chairs.

**RIGHT** The dining room's trompe l'oeil ceiling and candy-striped corner poles create a tented festival feel—"more flamboyant than our usual style," admits Smith, "but it certainly gives our dinner parties a sense of occasion."

**LEFT** "I have come to rely on the house as an invaluable design laboratory," says Smith, who designed the kitchen and breakfast room wallpaper "to bring a warm, fun atmosphere to what is probably our most-used room."

**ABOVE** Throughout the house, as in this bedroom, Smith repeats two themes: black and stripes. "I find they're best when combined," he says. The primary bedroom wallpaper was inspired by a Japanese screen.

# TRUE *to* FORM

A Connecticut Colonial shows off early American authenticity
thanks to a revolutionary revival by designer Philip Gorrivan.

**LEFT** "There's always a temptation when you have a blank slate to do interesting decorative things," says Gorrivan, who added simple millwork, window trim, and chair rails in this living room but otherwise kept "it closer to the way I thought it would have been."

**ABOVE** Gorrivan updated the kitchen with 1920s-era cabinets—still vintage but not Colonial—giving the home's historic vibe a more functional tweak. In the adjacent breakfast nook, horizontal wainscoting, painted a whispery gray, adds timeless detail.

**PAGE 164** New York-based Gorrivan had long been a fan of the Colonial gems in Washington, Connecticut, where he owns a 19th-century weekend home, so he relished the opportunity to restore this 1750 beauty—one of the area's oldest—for neighbors. "I've always admired its symmetry and scale. It's a perfect example of American Colonial architecture."

**PAGE 165** Despite its nostalgic appeal, the home was in need of a major overhaul. Gorrivan kept the front stairs—"a beautiful architectural element"—even though they were too steep to meet current code (rectified by adding new stairs in back).

**LEFT** A new bedroom added on to the rear of the house still honors the abode's sense of the past. Gorrivan chose a beadboard tray ceiling and installed a Gustavian alcove bed from the clients' former house, complete with intricate millwork, to amplify historic character.

**RIGHT** Gorrivan repurposed a 1920s bay window in the main bath, bringing brightness and garden tub views to the flower-wallpapered room. He infused a "fresh breath of life" without fussiness—witness the bathroom's simple sconces and classic white wainscoting.

**RIGHT** Another Gustavian bed in the guest room nods to the homeowner's Swedish heritage and adds flavor. "The painted pieces, in particular, lighten and add a level of sophistication to this antique American house," says Gorrivan.

"*The goal was to restore the house in a way that would make it last the next hundred years.*" —*Philip Gorrivan*

# RUSSIAN RIVER RENAISSANCE

In Healdsburg, California, designer Ken Fulk melds
subdued glamour with vintage soulfulness, rooting this
storied estate in its vineyard surroundings.

PAGES 170-171 For longtime clients who needed more room as their grown kids began having families of their own, Fulk created a multigenerational compound from a series of houses and barns on a storied wine country ranch—"a setting for family gatherings that would stand the test of time," he says.

LEFT "We gave the place some real soul," says Fulk, who covered the dining room walls of the Hill House property in a hand-painted mural with the tonal beauty of rammed earth. "Stone, steel, and wood combined with soft suedes, Belgian linens, and luxe velvets add warmth and comfort," he says.

LEFT A window-lined entryway and corridor bridges the owners' suite and the main wing of the house.

RIGHT The compound includes numerous enticing gathering spots, like this snug, textural lounge with painted wood veneer surrounding the fireplace and a strié pattern wallcovering by Phillip Jeffries.

**ABOVE** For the main ranch house, once owned by Hollywood icon Fred MacMurray, Fulk aimed to "bring back a sense of Old California." He replaced Sheetrock walls with board-and-batten and gave the dining room's hefty Spanish trestle table counterweight from green metal industrial pendants.

**LEFT** The large farmhouse-style kitchen with rustic oak countertops, antique brick floors, and an authentic Hoosier cabinet includes a flip-up window "reminiscent of a roadside diner, allowing the family to pull up a chair from the outside and join the kitchen conversation," Fulk says.

**LEFT** Twin rattan beds by Serena & Lily and an ornate antique mirror mix with instructional botanical prints, a vintage holdover with schoolhouse nostalgia.

**RIGHT** "Each bedroom was given its own movie or narrative thread inspired by famous films, plays, or photographs," says Fulk, who selected romantic wallpapers to further set the scene. Think *Rebel Without a Cause* in this guest room, where the motorcycle-leather bed frame is finished with aged brass nails.

**RIGHT** "Showstopping views stretch across seemingly endless vineyards with the Mayacamas Mountains painted in the distance," says Fulk of the property's easy-to-appreciate appeal.

*chapter five*

# ISLAND ENCHANTMENT

L ET'S JUST DIVE IN, shall we? Bright color and happy, laid-back whimsy are barometers of chic in these enchanting island homes—like the rich aqua splash of tropical de Gournay gorgeousness Amanda Lindroth wraps around a Bahamian kitchen, or the electric turquoise and zingy pink ceilings Kit Kemp lavishes on her Barbadian pavilions. "That strong sunshine just eats color," says Kemp, who serves up room after open-air room of happy-hued spaces.

Islands by their very nature are one-off, unique. And as the homes presented here demonstrate, well-honed island decor expresses that same distinct personality—what sails in Martha's Vineyard may not float on Harbour Island. Of course, there are overlapping ingredients—sand, saltiness, and expanses of water—but British Colonial vernacular inspires a different design approach than a cedar-shingled Rhode Island farmhouse. As we island-hop in these pages, however, one rule holds true: "Comfort is key, as are understatement and restraint," says designer Miles Redd. (Although when it comes to her beloved sailors' valentines, Lindroth begs off on restraint.)

Relish the cool, salty breeze, bask in the warm sunshine, and indulge in these island dreams, where, for example, designer Matthew Carter embraces quaint pecky cypress walls and gives stairs a wash of maritime blue in a Harbour Island cottage. On Martha's Vineyard, designer Markham Roberts blends the past and present, the funky and more refined, to update a New England classic. In the Abacos, Redd goes high tide with saturated blues; while in Rhode Island, he and architect Gil Schafer teach an old seaside barn some swanky new tricks. On lush Barbados, breezy outdoor entertaining and living is the whole point of Kemp's magical retreat, and in Baker's Bay, Lindroth reels in all sorts of wicker and wonder to augment that jaw-dropping jungle of de Gournay blues and greens. Oh, to be a castaway!

**LEFT** In the Bahamas, an inviting pool pavilion by designer Amanda Lindroth is in the vein of a Roman-meets-Hindu temple, filled with blue-and-white decor.

# SHELL SEEKERS

In Baker's Bay, Bahamas, designer Amanda Lindroth marries traditional
Bahamian decor with ample fancifulness and hints of romance.

**ABOVE** For this Baker's Bay abode, Lindroth leaned into her resident Bahamian love of quintessential island flavor, showcased here in a coatrack collage of market baskets and hats.

**LEFT** When California newlyweds fell for the pristine beaches of Baker's Bay, they engaged Lindroth to design their dream vacation home; she in turn partnered with architect Maria de la Guardia. Lindroth commissioned the sailor's valentine, the signature octagonal shell art of Caribbean seafarers, as a housewarming gift from the husband to his bride.

**PAGE 180** Though it's new construction, this Palladian coralina stone house is an ode to ancient principles of balance and harmony. "Why do I feel better in your rooms than others?" Lindroth queried de la Guardia. "It's not arbitrary. It's math and proportions," the Miami-based classicist replied.

**PAGE 181** A Tuscan-inspired loggia is ideal for de rigueur alfresco dining. "In the Bahamas it's plan B to be inside. Breakfast, lunch, and dinner are always eaten outdoors," says the architect.

**LEFT** Lindroth dubs the home's surrounding tangle of hibiscus, palms, bougainvillea, and banyans as "the jungle," and serves up similar lushness in the kitchen's turquoise rainforest, where de Gournay's Amazonia wallcovering dazzles.

**ABOVE** Lindroth loves how the lacquered mahogany breakfast table is "shiny, like a bar top," but the tailored and tufted poached-salmon banquette signals more of a swank tropical café.

**LEFT** A gently curving stairwell displays aquatic treasures—sponges, coral, and conch—alongside blue-and-white porcelain— a Lindroth favorite.

**RIGHT** In the primary bedroom, a draped canopy bed in Ralph Lauren sheers harks back to mosquito-netting days, while Indian-inspired paisley-stenciled walls hint at the island's British Colonial heritage.

**RIGHT** English artist Linda Fenwick created an enchanting shell-encased powder room, like a mermaid's lair.

"Once you hear the traditional Bahamian greeting
'Welcome home,' you are forever part of the place."

—Architect Maria de la Guardia

# SALTY SALUTE

Miles Redd and Gil Schafer reimagine a 19th-century farm
for a family of six, prioritizing sunlight and salt air,
and preserving a beloved landmark of summers past.

**ABOVE** A cedar-shingled farmhouse overlooking Great Salt Pond honors New England simplicity and Block Island's sense of community. Architecture by Schafer and design by Redd reenvisioned the 16-acre property for a Florida family who have summered there for decades.

**RIGHT** "Everything was about creating connections to the view and indoor/outdoor living," says Schafer, who maximized glass doors and windows opening to the waterfront, and bathed walls in a soft conch-shell pink.

LEFT "They're an active family, out and about on the land, on the water," but the home's numerous nooks and communal spaces, like this comfy library, "are generous, for the idea of gathering," says Redd.

LEFT Shades of sea and sky blue in the lacquer-and-brass lighting and the custom-marbled hallway mirror reinforce the outdoor connection.

RIGHT Sunshine and big views are this roomy kitchen's main ingredients. The island's pippy oak countertop gives an earthy contrast to the white marble elsewhere.

**LEFT** Sunny yellows and ocean blues summon bright beach days ahead when waking up in this cheerful guest bedroom.

**RIGHT** Over the garage, a guest suite with private balcony is anchored by a custom lemony linen sofa.

**RIGHT** Painted grass cloth walls "give texture but feel beachy and old-fashioned, like they've always been there," says Redd of the primary bedroom. Vintage florals and a painted desk add to the yesteryear softness.

*"Comfort is key, as are understatement and restraint."*

—Miles Redd

# BUOYANT BARBADOS

British hotelier and designer Kit Kemp invokes a welcoming spirit with an abundance of bright, playful patterns at her exotic yet at-ease Barbadian outpost.

**ABOVE** Kemp escapes to her colorful Barbados retreat, an overhaul of a 1950s hacienda, as often as possible. Open-air living and dining pavilions, with ceilings painted in pizzazzy pinks and blues, create a sense of luxury in the midst of tropical surroundings.

**LEFT** "We loved that the central pavilion was open on three sides, offering a constant breeze," says Kemp, a proponent of get-cozy ease. "I invite guests to take their shoes off, so they feel the texture underfoot and just relax," she adds, referencing the mix of old brick and hardwood floors, and of course, sandy beaches.

**PAGE 194** Kemp added 18th-century Indian doors to the breezeway. "They give a sense that the house has always been here," she says.

**PAGE 195** A poolside gazebo showcases Kemp's love of textiles and texture, including patterns she developed with Annie Selke, like in this quilted aqua geometric tablecloth and pillows popping with color.

◆

*"No matter how old you are, when you're here, sitting around the table with dear friends in the sunshine, people are the same age as when you first met them. Here, we're still young and happy."*

—*Kit Kemp*

# A VINEYARD CLASSIC

In a historic shingled retreat on Martha's Vineyard, designer Markham Roberts
weaves past and present with just enough beach house saltiness.

**LEFT** Roberts and architect Andrew Herdeg updated a traditional three-story Martha's Vineyard summer home, creating family-friendly spaces Roberts describes as "relevant and comfortable." In the kitchen and family room, indigos mix with beachy woven accents.

**ABOVE** Blue and plum hues add punch to the home's green-and-white palette. In island fashion (ferrying large pieces to and fro is avoided), the dining table was conveyed from previous owners.

**PAGE 200** Many furnishings, including the citrine foyer's Saarinen table and wire chandelier, were rescued from the homeowners' storage, remnants from the first apartment Markham designed for his then-newlywed clients decades ago.

**PAGE 201** A modern back porch helps "connect people to the landscape," says Herdeg, who kept supports thin "to emphasize the ocean views." A dark-stained woodfloor allows the porch to recede and "the traditional architecture to come forward."

"*You'll see 50,000 pairs of flip-flops in the summer, but we can have formal spaces in this house because most of the hard living happens on the porches or up on the third floor.*"

—*Markham Roberts*

**ABOVE** "The rooms don't have a lot of stuff in them—they're charming and quirky, like a beach house should be," says Roberts, who balances light and dark pieces, countering a linen floral upholstered bed with a vintage wicker rocker.

**RIGHT** Custom lattice cabinetry and the natural woven rug and wallcovering add coastal lightness to the upstairs study, where a 20th-century Danish desk takes center stage.

**BELOW** The home's cedar shingles, traditional shutters, and dormers represent classic Martha's Vineyard vernacular.

# HARBOURING DELIGHT

Designer Matthew Carter's long-held dream of a tropical getaway comes alive in this midcentury
Harbour Island cottage, invigorated by his love of color and texture.

**LEFT** The chic charm of Chanticleer Hill, a midcentury cottage wrapped in Chippendale railing, captivated Carter and his partner, architect Brent Bruner, at first sight, some 18 years before they eventually bought and restored it.

**RIGHT** "Horrified" by the 70-year-old cottage's poor condition, Carter and Bruner opened up rooms, added a guest cottage, and infused imaginative details, like a Moorish arch between the dining and living rooms. "I took my pencil, climbed a ladder, and drew it on the wall. I could picture it. Luckily our contractor never said no," says Carter.

PAGE 206 The blush pink, palm-graced veranda, with columns framed in British Colonial flourish, welcomes year-round outdoor living and entertaining.

PAGE 207 "Deep greens, dark browns, and a whole lot of white: This combination feels elegantly organic to me," says Carter. The stairwell gallery of midcentury Bahamas and Florida photos underscores the vintage tropical vibe.

LEFT Local materials— mahogany countertops, Abaco pine beams, and coralina stone floors— keep the kitchen flavor island-authentic.

**LEFT** In the den, a 1970s coconut shell coffee table amplifies the room's chocolaty accents, contrasted with a spirited raspberry burst in the contemporary artwork.

**ABOVE** The quadrille pattern on the den's pillows is first introduced via the entryway slipper chair, where an antique Italian lantern and streamlined Saarinen table offer a yin-yang form.

**LEFT** Alfresco breakfast on the cottage's sunny terrace is one of the perks of Harbour Island's down-to-earth appeal.

**ABOVE** After sensing the primary bedroom was "missing something," Carter painted the beams a sassy chartreuse, "a lovely, weird green that doesn't exist anywhere else in the room," says the designer, who loves the cotton Mexican coverlet's "salt- and sun-bleached" feel.

# BAHAMIAN RHAPSODY

Designer Miles Redd, a master at conjuring modern rooms juiced with personality, brings the blues (and reds) to a California family's Abaco escape.

PAGES 214-215 Colonial-era columns and rooflines extending like "the broad brim of a hat" are among the Abaco-esque details that architect Jacki Yahn incorporated into this waterfront home. Redd did interiors as well as the poolside, where white monochrome simplicity defers to the landscape. "Don't try to compete with nature," Redd advises.

LEFT "Art helps a room feel complete and can make soft colors feel less wan and stronger colors appear more mellow," says Redd. The living room's sun-and-sky palette is mirrored by outdoor island vistas thanks to ample French doors.

LEFT "I like putting something raw next to something slick, something nacreous next to something rough," says Redd, who jazzes the entryway with zigzags, chevron stripes, and Chinese porcelain against grass cloth walls.

RIGHT By shifting storage to an adjacent anteroom, Redd frees up the kitchen walls for gallery space, making the room "feel like an extension of the living room."

**LEFT** The polished 20th-century dining table, a find from Christie's, is a reward from Redd's habit of "hitting every auction and market I can to find interesting, unusual pieces."

**RIGHT** Redd goes full tilt in this powder keg of a powder room. By taking it "over the top in these little spaces, you take people's breath away," the fearless designer says.

**ABOVE** Classic peacock wicker headboards and rattan sconces stand out amid lively pink-patterned walls. Redd painted a concentric square pattern on rush benches to convert a catalog item into a custom piece.

*"My cry to myself is, 'Don't make things too fancy,' but I love fancy."*
—Miles Redd

# INDEX

**STEPHANIE HUNT** is a writer in Charleston, South Carolina, and a regular contributor to VERANDA. A native Southerner, she writes about style and design and community and culture for a number of publications, including *Coastal Living, Southern Living, Luxe, The Washington Post,* and *Charleston Magazine.*

**STEELE THOMAS MARCOUX** is the editor of VERANDA and a veteran of the design publishing industry, having served in senior editorial roles at *Country Living, Coastal Living,* and *Southern Living.* She is a member of the board of directors of the Alabama School of Fine Arts in Birmingham, Alabama, where she lives with her husband, two sons, and two dogs.

# PHOTOGRAPHY CREDITS

**Ricardo Labougle** cover: Artwork © 2022 Artists Rights Society (ARS), New York / SIAE, Rome, 20–27
**Dylan Thomas** 1, 40–45, 156–163
**Lisa Romerein** 2–3, 58, 60–65
**Thomas Loof** 4, 7, 10–19, 34–39, 74–79
**Annie Schlechter** 8, 66–73, 104–111, 132–139, 194–199

**Paul Costello** 28–33
**Bjorn Wallander** 46–51
**Stephen Kent Johnson** 52–57
**Francesco Lagnese** 80–85
**Eric Piasecki** 86–95, 188–193
**William Abranowicz/Art + Commerce** 96, 98–103
**Simon Upton** 112–117
**Douglas Friedman** 118–125, 170–177

**Victoria Pearson** 126–131
**James McDonald** 140, 142–149
**Max Kim-Bee** 150–155
**Joshua McHugh** 164–169
**Miguel Flores-Vianna** 178, 180–187
**Nelson Hancock** 200–205
**Brie Williams** 206–213
**Melanie Acevado** back cover, 214–219

**HEARST**
**HOME**

Cover and book design by Erynn Hassinger

Library of Congress Cataloging-in-
Publication Data Available on Request

10 9 8 7 6 5 4 3 2 1

Published by Hearst Home, an imprint of Hearst
Books/Hearst Communications, Inc.

Hearst Magazine Media, Inc.

300 West 57th Street
New York, New York 10019

VERANDA, Hearst Home, the Hearst Home
logo, and Hearst Books are registered
trademarks of Hearst Communications, Inc.

For information about custom editions,
special sales, premium and corporate
purchases: hearst.com/magazines/
hearst-books

Printed in China

ISBN 978-1-958395-86-8